ENERGY TODAY

Geothermal Energy

by Alan Wachtel

Science and Curriculum Consultant:
Debra Voege, M.A.,
Science Curriculum Resource Teacher

CHELSEA CLUBHOUSE
An Imprint of Chelsea House Publishers

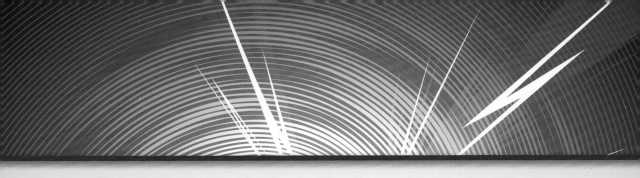

Energy Today: Geothermal Energy

Copyright © 2010 by Infobase Publishing

Chelsea Clubhouse
An imprint of Chelsea House Publishers
132 West 31st Street
New York NY 10001

Library of Congress Cataloging-in-Publication Data
Wachtel, Alan.
     Geothermal energy / by Alan Wachtel.
        p. cm. — (Energy today)
     Includes bibliographical references and index.
     ISBN 978-1-60413-786-6
     1. Geothermal power plants—Juvenile literature.
     2. Geothermal resources—Juvenile literature. I. Title. II. Series.
   TK1055.W33 2010
   333.8'8—dc22   2009044614

Chelsea Clubhouse books are available at special discounts when purchased in bulk quantities for businesses, associations, institutions, or sales promotions. Please call our Special Sales Department in New York at (212) 967-8800 or (800) 322-8755.

You can find Chelsea Clubhouse on the World Wide Web at http://www.chelseahouse.com

Developed for Chelsea House by RJF Publishing LLC (www.RJFpublishing.com)
Project Editor: Jacqueline Laks Gorman
Text and cover design by Tammy West/Westgraphix LLC
Illustrations by Spectrum Creative Inc.
Photo research by Edward A. Thomas
Index by Nila Glikin
Composition by Westgraphix LLC
Cover printed by Bang Printing, Brainerd, MN
Book printed and bound by Bang Printing, Brainerd, MN
Date printed: May 2010
Printed in the United States of America

Photo Credits: 6: Paul Thompson/Imagestate RM/Photolibrary; 7: (top) Douglas Peebles/Photolibrary, (bottom) © Robert Malone/Alamy; 10: iStockphoto; 13: Richard Rasmussen/America 24-7/Getty Images; 17: © naglestock.com/Alamy; 22: AP Images; 23: Courtesy of Geo-Heat Center/NREL; 25: Thomas McDonald/The New York Times; 27: © GlowImages/Alamy; 28: Nicole Bengiveno/The New York Times/Redux; 31: KEVIN SCHAFER/Peter Arnold Inc.; 33: Courtesy of Arizona Public Service/NREL–Carol Shipman; 34: Lionel Mestre, 2008, All rights reserved; 35: Gerald & Buff Corsi/Visuals Unlimited, Inc.; 36: CHRISTIAN FLIERL/The New York Times; 40: (top) AP Images, (bottom) Rina Castelnuovo/The New York Times; 41: JIM WILSON/The New York Times; 42: Courtesy of NREL.

10 9 8 7 6 5 4 3 2 1

TABLE OF CONTENTS

CHAPTER 1:
Earth Power 4

CHAPTER 2:
From the Core to the Socket 12

CHAPTER 3:
A Clean Energy Source 24

CHAPTER 4:
Geothermal Drawbacks 32

CHAPTER 5:
Geothermal Tomorrow 38

Glossary.. 44

To Learn More.. 46

Index...47

Words that are defined in the Glossary are in **bold** type the first time they appear in the text.

Earth Power

Geothermal energy is energy that comes from deep inside of Earth. The word geothermal comes from the Greek words *geo* (meaning "earth") and *therme* (meaning "heat"). Geothermal power is a clean, **renewable** energy source that may someday provide a significant portion of the world's energy.

What Is Geothermal Energy?

At the center of Earth—about 4,000 miles (6,400 kilometers) below the surface—is a very hot **core**. Some scientists estimate its temperature at about 7600° Fahrenheit (4200° Celsius). The center of the core is solid. The heat from this part of the core is powerful enough to melt rock into a hot liquid called **magma**. This molten (melted) rock forms the outer core. The heat from magma rises through Earth's **mantle**. The mantle is the layer that surrounds the core.

Geothermal energy powers volcanoes, **geysers**, and natural **hot springs**. Erupting volcanoes are probably the most famous geothermal events. When a volcano erupts, magma from underground shoots through Earth's crust and flows onto its surface as lava. Over time, people have learned to use geothermal energy to heat homes and produce electricity.

Today, geothermal energy is more important than ever. People around the world use a great deal of energy—to heat

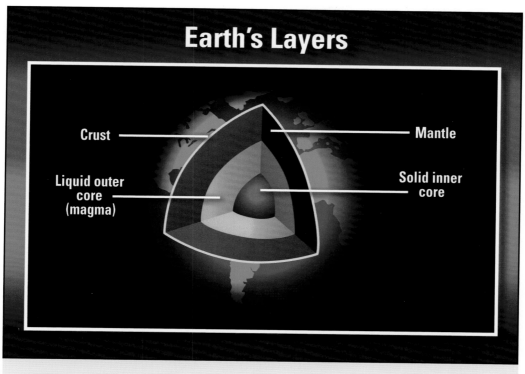

Earth's Layers

Crust — — Mantle

Liquid outer core (magma) — — Solid inner core

Geothermal energy comes from deep inside Earth, in the core, where temperatures reach thousands of degrees.

homes, to take hot showers, to fuel cars, and to generate the electricity that powers everything from electric lights to factories to home computers. As more countries of the world develop, more people keep using more electricity. More energy will be needed. As people look for new sources of energy, many think geothermal energy will play a big role in the future.

Use of Geothermal Energy Today

Geothermal energy is already used all over the world. It is used directly in more than 70 countries. "Direct use" means that heat energy straight from Earth is used to heat a house or other building. People can use geothermal energy directly only

Geysers—such as this one in New Zealand—are springs that shoot hot water and steam into the air.

in areas where the energy naturally reaches the surface. In the United States, most direct use of geothermal energy is in the western states.

As of 2008, 24 countries were using geothermal energy to generate electricity. The world's biggest users of such electricity are the United States, the Philippines, Indonesia, Mexico, Italy, Japan, New Zealand, and Iceland. The United States produces more geothermal energy than any other country—30 percent of the world's total. The country uses so much power overall, however, that geothermal energy plays only a small role. In 2007, it accounted for only 5 percent of all the renewable energy used in the United States. In the United States, geothermal energy lagged behind certain other renewable energy sources. Water power and **biofuels** both produced more power than geothermal sources.

Some smaller countries get higher percentages of their power from geothermal sources. The Philippines is the second-largest producer of geothermal energy. It gets 27 percent of its electricity from geothermal sources. Iceland, a country with only about 300,000 people, gets 20 percent of its electricity from geothermal sources. Even more impressive, geothermal energy heats approximately 90 percent of homes in Iceland.

When a volcano erupts, magma from underground shoots through Earth's crust and flows onto the surface.

As striking as these numbers sound, geothermal energy accounts for very little of the world's energy. Geothermal energy makes up only 0.4 percent of the world's energy production. In all, the world generates only about 10,000 **megawatts** of geothermal energy. The Geothermal Energy Association (a group of U.S. companies that support the use of geothermal energy) says that this is enough power to meet the needs of 60 million people. The population of the world is currently about 6.7 billion, so this represents only a small portion of the world's people.

The Importance of New Energy Sources

Finding new sources of energy is important. The U.S. government predicts that world energy use will

Hot steam escapes from a geothermal facility in Iceland, a country that gets a great deal of its energy from geothermal sources.

Did You Know?
Geothermal Alaska

The state of Alaska is one of the biggest producers of oil and gas in the United States. It is also rich in geothermal resources. Alaska's geothermal resources have been known for a long time. Alaska stopped developing geothermal energy in the 1970s, however, after major new deposits of oil were found in the state. In 2004, a company called United Technologies Corporation teamed up with Chena Hot Springs, a resort located in Fairbanks. The partners began using geothermal energy to make electricity in Alaska in 2006. In another project, in 2008, Naknek Electric Association began drilling a geothermal exploration well near King Salmon, Alaska. (This type of well is drilled to see what type of resources exist.) Ten years of research and planning went into the project. It may provide 25 megawatts of power—enough for 28 villages in Alaska.

increase by almost 30 percent between 2006 and 2030. Demand for energy is growing fastest in large **developing countries**, such as China and India. Demand is also growing in developed countries, such as the United States. The developed countries are already the world's top energy users.

Fossil fuels, such as coal, oil, and natural gas, are the most popular energy sources around the world today. Over the next few decades, the demand for fossil fuels is expected to rise. The production of fossil fuels is also expected to rise, but the supply of fossil fuels is limited. These fuels started out as plants and animals that lived millions of years ago. After these plants and animals died, they decomposed (broke down) under layers of soil and rock. Over millions of years, their remains changed into materials such as coal, oil, and natural gas. Once we have used up all of the fossil fuels that are currently under Earth's surface, there will be no more fossil fuels to replace them.

The world is also looking for cleaner and safer sources of energy. In the United States and elsewhere around the world, many **power plants** run on coal and oil. Coal and oil release harmful substances into the air when they are burned. For this reason, many people would like to see power plants use cleaner sources of energy.

After fossil fuels, **nuclear** power is the next most used source of energy in the United States, but its use is **controversial**. Many people oppose nuclear power plants because they believe that the plants and the **radioactive waste** associated with them are dangerous. Many people who oppose the use of

Did You Know?

Old Faithful

Old Faithful is a famous geyser in Yellowstone National Park, which is located in Wyoming, Montana, and Idaho. The park is located on an area of great geothermal activity. Old Faithful is actually one of more than 300 geysers in Yellowstone. It erupts about every 1 to 1½ hours. When Old Faithful erupts, a stream of water shoots into the air. It can shoot as high as 184 feet (56 meters)! The water is very hot. Just before Old Faithful erupts, the water beneath the ground is more than 200°F (93°C)—boiling hot!

Did You Know?

Global Warming

Earth's **climate** is getting warmer, and many scientists think the rise in climate temperatures around the globe may have serious effects. Many scientists think, for example, that climate change is causing a melting of the ice in the regions around the North and South Poles. This may lead to a rise in sea levels, which could increase the possibility of floods in coastal areas and on islands.

Many scientists believe that Earth's temperatures are increasing because of human activity. Burning fossil fuels releases the gas **carbon dioxide** into the **atmosphere**. Carbon dioxide traps heat in the atmosphere, so burning fossil fuels leads to rising temperatures. Many scientists think that turning to power sources such as geothermal energy, instead of continuing to use fossil fuels, can help prevent a **catastrophe**.

Power plants that burn coal release harmful substances into the air.

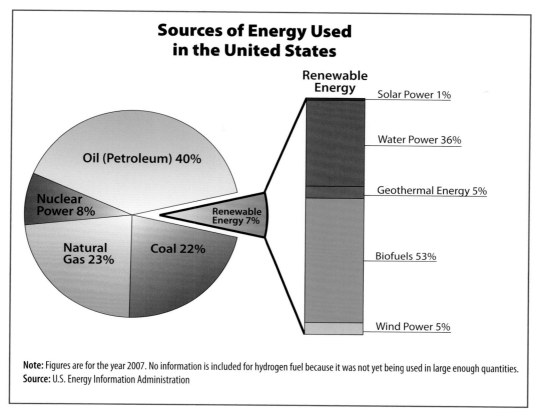

Sources of Energy Used in the United States

Oil (Petroleum) 40%

Nuclear Power 8%

Natural Gas 23%

Coal 22%

Renewable Energy 7%

Renewable Energy
- Solar Power 1%
- Water Power 36%
- Geothermal Energy 5%
- Biofuels 53%
- Wind Power 5%

Note: Figures are for the year 2007. No information is included for hydrogen fuel because it was not yet being used in large enough quantities.
Source: U.S. Energy Information Administration

fossil fuels and nuclear energy believe geothermal energy is a clean and safe alternative.

Earth Power for the Future

Between 2005 and 2007, world output of geothermal energy increased by 800 megawatts. This increase is part of a trend. Since the 1980s, output of geothermal energy has increased between 200 and 250 megawatts each year. In addition, in 2006, scientists from the Massachusetts Institute of Technology published a report about geothermal energy. They said that the United States has vast geothermal resources. They also said that improvements in geothermal energy technology could give the country access to **sustainable** power for thousands of years.

CHAPTER 2

From the Core to the Socket

The use of geothermal energy began before history was recorded. More than 10,000 years ago, early Native Americans used hot springs for cooking and bathing. Ancient Romans in Italy used hot springs for cooking, bathing, and heating their homes. Since that time, geothermal energy has been put to other uses as well.

More Recent History

In the nineteenth century, when settlers in North America moved west, they discovered hot springs. In 1807, the explorer John Colter found hot water coming up from the ground. He was on land that is now part of Yellowstone National Park. That same year, the city of Hot Springs, Arkansas, was founded. Hot Springs has 47 natural springs. The water coming from these springs is about 143°F (62°C). Native Americans had been using the springs there for centuries. In 1832, Hot Springs became the first federally protected area in the United States. Today, it is the only U.S. city that has a national park—Hot Springs National Park—almost entirely within the city limits.

In 1852, a spa—a resort where people relax and have treatments to improve their health—opened at the Geysers, north of San Francisco, California. This location is known for natural hot springs. (Its name is not quite accurate, because the area does not contain any actual geysers.) Over the years, famous figures such as President Theodore Roosevelt, businessman J. P. Morgan, and writer Mark Twain visited the Geysers Resort Hotel.

In 1864, the Hot Lake Hotel opened near La Grande, Oregon. This hotel represented the first use of geothermal energy to heat a large building. By 1892, Boise, Idaho, had the first **district** heating system in the United States, with water piped in from nearby hot springs to heat buildings in the town. Within a few years, 200 homes and 40 businesses in Boise were heated by water from the springs. Today, more than 5 million square feet (464,500 square meters) of homes, businesses, and government buildings in Boise are part of the district system.

Commercial and industrial use of geothermal energy began in the early twentieth century. The first geothermal power

Steam rises from a spring at Hot Springs National Park in Arkansas.

In Their Own Words

"The huge reservoir of volcanic energy represented by the heat of rocks and gases could undoubtedly be tapped in many places and used for power production.... I believe that in time to come the greatest of all sources of power will be found in the subterranean [underground] storehouses of volcanic regions, where the internal heat of the earth can be reached."

Scientist Immanuel Friedlander, 1928

plant in the world opened in Larderello, Italy, in 1913. In 1922, the first geothermal power plant in the United States opened near the Geysers. The developer had to dig a number of wells to bring up enough steam to use to produce electricity. (A well is a hole that is drilled to find or produce something like oil, natural gas, or a source of geothermal heat.) The plant at the Geysers did not produce much power. In 1930, a man named Charlie Lieb invented a **device** called a downhole heat exchanger, or DHE. The DHE enabled direct use of geothermal energy to heat a house. Another important device, the ground-source heat pump, was invented in 1948 by an Ohio State University professor named Carl Nielsen. Nielsen used the pump to heat and cool his house.

In 1960, a successful geothermal power plant was built at the Geysers. That particular plant ran for more than 30 years. By the middle of the twentieth century, it was clear that geothermal energy was here to stay.

Did You Know?

Power at the Geysers

The first large-scale commercial geothermal power plant in the United States opened at the Geysers, in California, in 1960. The original power plant produced 11 megawatts of electricity. By 1989, the Geysers had 23 geothermal power plants. The Geysers is currently the world's largest source of geothermal energy. In 2007, Calpine—one of the companies that operates plants at the Geysers—began a project to increase geothermal power production there by 80 megawatts.

How Geothermal Energy Works

Geothermal energy works in three main ways. All take advantage of the heat beneath Earth's surface—either close to the surface or deep below. The first way is *direct geothermal energy*, using hot water that is at or near Earth's surface. The second way is *geothermal heat pumps*, using water that is below the ground but not too deep. The third way is *geothermal power plants*, using hot water and steam from deep underground to generate electricity.

Direct Geothermal Energy

In some places, hot water naturally comes up to or close to Earth's surface. Naturally heated hot water that comes to the

JOHN COLTER

Little is known about John Colter's life. He was born in Virginia around the year 1774, and he and his family moved to Kentucky a few years later. Some of Colter's adventures as an explorer are famous. In 1803, he joined the team of the explorers Meriwether Lewis and William Clark. With Lewis and Clark, Colter traveled from Kentucky through the Rocky Mountains to the Pacific Ocean. Then, the group turned back. On the return trip, in North Dakota, Colter separated from Lewis and Clark's team. He then teamed up with some fur trappers and headed west again. Eventually, in 1807, Colter found his way to what is now Yellowstone National Park. Many people believe that he was the first white man to visit this area. Colter's description of the land included stories of steam, smoke, and smelly gases that escaped from the ground. As a result, some people called the area he described "Colter's Hell." Colter died in 1813.

surface is called a hot spring. Naturally heated underground **reservoirs** are called geothermal reservoirs. People have used this type of hot water for centuries.

In places that have hot springs or geothermal reservoirs, people use simple systems to take advantage of the heat. In this direct use of geothermal energy, hot water flows from a source (such as a well) into a building's heating system. The temperature of the water can range from about 68°F to 302°F (20°C to 150°C). The heating system uses what is called a heat exchanger—a device that can transfer heat from one medium to another, such as from water to air. One example of a heat exchanger is a radiator. The radiator releases the heat—but not the hot water—into the building. Pipes then carry the water back underground. There, the water is heated once more and can be used again to provide more energy.

Did You Know?

Larderello:
The First Geothermal Energy Plant

Larderello is located in a part of Italy that is volcanic (tends to have volcanoes). The last eruption there occurred in the thirteenth century. Long after that time, steam and hot water continued to come up through the ground. In 1904, Prince Piero Ginori Conti used Larderello's natural steam to generate a small amount of electricity. This was the first time geothermal energy was ever used to make electricity. Some years later, the world's first geothermal power plant opened in Larderello's Valle del Diavolo (which means "Devil's Valley"). For some 50 years, it remained the world's only geothermal power plant. It continues to produce power today. It is not, however, as productive as it once was. In 2003, scientists said its underground reserves had dropped 30 percent from their peak in the 1950s. Still, about one million homes today get their electricity from Larderello's geothermal energy.

The geothermal power plant at Larderello, which is located in northern Italy.

Geothermal Heat Pumps

People also harness geothermal energy by using heat-pump systems. These systems take advantage of stable temperatures beneath Earth's surface. No matter what season it is, a few feet underground, the temperature is about 50°F to 60°F (10°C to 15°C).

Heat-pump systems include three parts: what is called an Earth connection, the heat pump itself, and a heat distribution system. The Earth connection is a loop of pipes buried in the ground near or beneath a building. A fluid circulates in the loop of pipes. The fluid is water or a mixture of water and **antifreeze**. The fluid picks up heat from within Earth. The heat pump removes heat from the fluid and sends it to the building. Then, pipes distribute the heat through the building. When it is warm out, heat-pump systems can be used backwards for cooling. The system pulls warm air from the building and sends it underground.

Geothermal Power Plants

Geothermal energy is also used to generate electricity. Hydrothermal systems—which use hot water or steam from underground—convert energy from Earth's heat into electricity. There are three main kinds of hydrothermal systems in use: dry-steam power plants, flash-steam power plants, and binary-cycle power plants. All three of these systems harness the power of hydrothermal fluid—that is, water or steam—that is naturally heated within Earth.

Dry-steam power plants take steam inside Earth and use it to drive a **turbine**. Geothermal reservoirs filled with steam

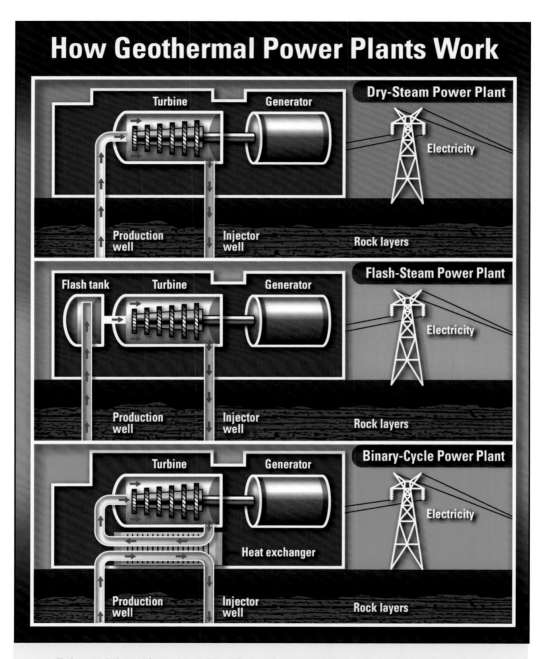

How Geothermal Power Plants Work

Dry-Steam Power Plant

Turbine

Generator

Electricity

Production well

Injector well

Rock layers

Flash-Steam Power Plant

Flash tank

Turbine

Generator

Electricity

Production well

Injector well

Rock layers

Binary-Cycle Power Plant

Turbine

Generator

Electricity

Heat exchanger

Production well

Injector well

Rock layers

In all three of the major types of geothermal power plants, steam, hot water, or vapor is used to drive a turbine. This powers a generator, which produces electricity.

Did You Know?
Geothermal Energy
Around the World

Geothermal energy is an important source of power in the Philippines and Iceland. In addition to these nations, other countries that make significant use of geothermal energy include New Zealand and Papua New Guinea. Both are island nations located in Oceania. One major use of geothermal energy in Papua New Guinea is to provide power for operating a large gold mine on Lihir Island. Much of New Zealand's geothermal resources are located in its Northland region. The many geothermal power plants in this region include dry-steam, flash-steam, and binary-cycle plants.

exist inside Earth. First, a well is drilled to reach the steam. The steam rises through the well. As it rises, it spins the **rotors** of the turbine. The turbine is connected to a **generator**. Electricity produced by the generator can be carried by wires to wherever people need it. Dry-steam power plants were the first type of geothermal power plant.

Flash-steam power plants are similar to dry-steam power plants. Instead of using natural steam, however, they use naturally hot—very hot—water. The temperature of the water used in flash-steam power plants ranges from 300°F to 700°F (150°C to 370°C). Underground, there is great pressure that keeps the water in liquid form at temperatures far higher than its usual boiling point. The hot water comes up to the surface through a well. At the surface, it is sprayed into a tank. The tank is kept at much lower pressure than the geothermal fluid. When the very hot water hits the tank, it vaporizes (turns to steam) in a "flash" of energy. The flash of energy turns the rotors of a turbine, which is connected to an electrical generator. Some flash-steam power plants use more than one tank. If there is still hot water in the first tank, it can be flashed again in the second tank, taking advantage of all the heat energy. When the steam cools down, it changes back into water. The water can be forced back into the ground to be used again. Flash-steam power plants are the most common type of geothermal plants in use today.

Binary-cycle power plants are more complicated. The water they use is considered moderately hot—below 400°F (200°C). In these power plants, the hot water does not directly turn the turbine. Instead, as the water comes above ground from a well, it enters a heat exchanger. The heat exchanger transfers the geothermal heat to a different fluid that has a lower boiling point. This second fluid then flashes into **vapor**, which turns the turbine. After it turns the turbine, the second fluid flows back into the heat exchanger.

In the future, some binary-cycle power plants will generate electricity using what are called enhanced geothermal systems, or EGS. (They are also sometimes called engineered geothermal systems.) Most geothermal energy systems today depend on natural geothermal reservoirs. Enhanced geothermal systems are different because they use an artificial (manufactured) geothermal reservoir. Many people believe that even in places with no natural geothermal reservoirs, there are great resources of geothermal energy. EGS projects would take advantage of that energy. Deep beneath Earth's surface is hot, dry rock. First, a well is drilled approximately 2 to 6 miles (3 to 10 kilometers) into the rock. Then, water is injected into the well at very high pressure. The injected water leads to what is called hydrofracture, which is the breaking up of mostly solid hot rock to create an artificial reservoir. (This process is sometimes called stimulating geothermal energy.) The water becomes hot from contact with the hot rock. Then, more wells are drilled to bring the hot water to the surface. The hot water then provides the power for binary-cycle power plants.

Main Uses of Geothermal Energy

Currently, the most widespread use of geothermal energy is for heating. Geothermal energy heats homes, offices, greenhouses, fish farms, factories, and mines. It is also used for heating pools

The Ouray Hot Springs Pool in Colorado is heated with water that is piped in from a nearby geothermal well.

The streets of Klamath Falls, Oregon, are kept clear of snow because of an underground network of tubes containing hot water.

and drying agricultural products. Some cities—such as Klamath Falls, Oregon—pipe hot water under the sidewalks and roads to melt snow.

At the Ouray Hot Springs Pool in Ouray, Colorado, there is direct use of geothermal energy. This outdoor pool, located in the Colorado Rockies, measures 250 feet by 150 feet (76 meters by 46 meters). It is heated with water piped from a nearby geothermal well. The temperature of the pool is adjusted by balancing water from the geothermal well with water from another source. The pool is even open in the winter.

In some places, geothermal energy heats an entire district. One such place is the town of Philip, South Dakota. Philip is located above the Madison Formation. The Madison Formation is a large **aquifer** that contains naturally hot water. Eight buildings in Philip are heated with geothermal energy, including schools and a bank. An example of a building that uses a geothermal heat pump is the Greenburgh Public Library in Elmsford, New York, which opened in January 2009. The library uses geothermal energy to heat about 45,000 square feet (4,180 square meters) of space.

CHAPTER 3

A Clean Energy Source

One of the greatest advantages of geothermal energy is that it is widely available. The western United States is particularly rich in geothermal resources. The states of Washington, Oregon, California, Nevada, Utah, Idaho, Wyoming, Arizona, Montana, and New Mexico all have sites where heat not too far below Earth's surface exceeds 212°F (100°C). Almost the whole state of Nevada has such resources. In addition, the states of Alaska and Hawaii have significant geothermal resources.

These are not the only places in the United States that have great resources. Some states in the East also have them. Western New York, western Pennsylvania, and spots in West Virginia, North Carolina, Arkansas, and Delaware have notable geothermal resources.

Large-scale geothermal resources exist throughout the world. Anywhere that has volcanic activity has geothermal resources. Also, many regions near the boundaries (edges) of Earth's **plates** have geothermal resources. Plates are large sections of Earth's crust and upper mantle that move. As the boundaries of the plates move against each other, some sections of the crust buckle, while other sections rise. Hot magma sometimes enters the gap between plates, leading to the formation of a volcano. The western United States, the Philippines, Japan, and Indonesia are all near plate boundaries.

Available Anywhere, Anytime

Geothermal heat pumps can be used almost anywhere. The temperature a few feet below Earth's surface is about the same everywhere: 50°F to 60°F (10°C to 15°C). These temperatures are warm enough to help with heating in cold months. They can also help with cooling in hot months. Some people think that enhanced geothermal systems also can be used almost anywhere that wells can be drilled deeply—and safely—enough.

Not only is some kind of geothermal energy available almost anywhere, it is available almost anytime. Unlike other alternative energy sources, such as solar or wind power, geothermal energy is available whether or not the Sun is shining or the wind is blowing. All types of energy systems require some maintenance to keep them working well, but geothermal systems do not require very much. Direct geothermal energy and heat-pump systems need little maintenance and no additional fuel. Geothermal power plants are able to work and produce electricity 90 percent or more of the time. In contrast, coal-fueled power plants work only 75 percent of the time.

A Connecticut home owner checks the geothermal system in his house.

Did You Know?

The Ring of Fire

The rim of the Pacific Ocean is called the Ring of Fire because of all the volcanic activity in the area. Earthquakes are also common there. The volcanoes and earthquakes in the Ring of Fire occur because the edges of some of Earth's plates are in the region. At these plate boundaries, magma reaches Earth's surface and spews out through volcanoes. Volcanoes are a sign that geothermal energy is close to Earth's surface. It is no coincidence that the Ring of Fire borders some of the most geothermally active areas on Earth.

The Ring of Fire along the rim of the Pacific Ocean is the scene of frequent earthquakes and volcanoes.

Sustainable and Renewable

Geothermal energy is sustainable. The heat from within Earth is in no danger of running out. In addition to this, geothermal systems recycle the underground water that they use. After naturally hot water is piped up and its heat

One of the geothermal power plants at the Geysers in California.

transferred, the water is sent back underground, where it picks up heat again. This process makes geothermal energy renewable.

Geothermal power plants can have long life spans. The world's first geothermal power plant, located at Larderello, Italy, has been running since 1913—almost 100 years. In addition, the Geysers, in California, has been producing electricity for about 50 years. Although the geothermal waters in these places are not as strong as they once were, both sites are still valuable. At the Geysers, operators now reinject water to help keep pressure strong in the reservoirs.

Economic Advantages

Once people have installed the necessary equipment to use geothermal energy to heat their homes, they can save a lot of money. They do not have to pay for oil or natural gas to fuel their heating systems. Using a geothermal heat pump, it is possible in the United States to heat a 3,000-square-foot (280-square-meter) house for about $60 per month. This can be much less than

Did You Know?

Geothermal Energy in the Big City

In the United States, geothermal energy is not just for the western states, where it plentiful. It is even used right in the middle of New York City. About 60 sites in the city are heated by naturally hot water that runs beneath the city. Using wells that are between 1,500 and 1,800 feet (460 and 550 meters) deep, these sites use pumps to bring the hot water to buildings. One of these buildings is the General Theological Seminary of the Episcopal Church, which has owned the land on which the Seminary stands since the nineteenth century. In 2008, the Seminary installed 7 geothermal wells and had plans to drill 15 more. Maureen Burnley, the executive vice president of the Seminary, said, "We wanted to come into the twenty-first century. . . . We skipped the twentieth century altogether."

Some of the equipment at New York's General Theological Seminary.

the cost of heating a house of the same size with conventional energy. Many users of geothermal heat pumps save 30 to 60 percent on their energy bills each year, compared to the cost of heat from a fossil fuel source. A geothermal heat pump can be fairly expensive to buy and install, but the savings on energy costs are great enough that the pump can pay for itself in 5 to 10 years.

The use of geothermal energy by cities can also save a lot of money. The city of Lincoln, Nebraska, installed geothermal heat pumps in four elementary schools in 1995, using the heat pumps for both heating and cooling. The city's energy bills for the schools were 57 percent lower than the costs for two other schools that had traditional heating and cooling systems installed at the same time.

Another economic advantage of geothermal energy is that it creates jobs. A 2007 report said that if the United States added 5,635 megawatts of geothermally generated electricity, it would have to add almost 30,000 full-time jobs in constructing and operating the power plants. Because most of the geothermal resources in the United States are in rural areas, growth in geothermal energy could bring great benefit to places where there are few jobs. On top of this, the taxes collected from companies producing geothermal energy could also help rural communities.

Environmental Advantages

Burning fossil fuels releases carbon dioxide and other pollutants into the air. These pollutants have a bad effect on the planet. They have been linked to **acid rain** and global warming. They also harm the quality of the air that we breathe, causing such

Did You Know?

Energy Independence for the United States

The United States produces a great deal of coal, oil, and natural gas. The country, however, has a huge appetite for energy. It uses more energy than it produces. To satisfy its appetite, the United States must import (bring in) fuel from other countries. The main type of fuel that the United States imports is oil. Much of the oil the country imports comes from OPEC (Organization of Petroleum Exporting Countries). OPEC is a group of countries that work together to try to control the price of oil. Because the United States uses so much foreign oil, OPEC has a great influence on the price of energy in the United States.

The United States and some of the OPEC countries disagree on various political issues. Since the United States gets so much oil from OPEC nations, the United States sometimes must consider how those countries might react before it takes international political action that some OPEC members would disagree with. If the United States used more geothermal energy, it would bring the country closer to being able to meet its own energy needs. The more the United States could meet its own energy needs, the more independently it might be able to act in international politics.

Geothermal power plants release mainly steam, rather than harmful substances.

problems as asthma and pneumonia. Natural gas is one of the cleanest fossil fuels. Burning natural gas releases relatively little pollution into the atmosphere. Geothermal sources, however, are even cleaner. Geothermal sources do give off a small amount of carbon dioxide, but only one-sixth the amount that is given off by power plants that burn natural gas. Geothermal power plants release very few **emissions** or none at all. Flash-steam power plants give off only some excess steam. Binary-cycle power plants are completely "closed," which means that they make no contact with the atmosphere. They do not give off any emissions.

In California in the area surrounding the Geysers, the geothermal power plants have even helped the air quality. Hot springs naturally emit hydrogen sulfide, which is a foul-smelling gas. The power plants include a system that reduces emissions of hydrogen sulfide by 99 percent.

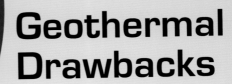

Geothermal Drawbacks

Geothermal energy has many benefits, but there are drawbacks. One of the most notable problems is the expense involved.

Difficult and Expensive

One of the biggest drawbacks involved with geothermal energy is that it is expensive to get started. For example, drilling a well for a geothermal power plant can cost $1 million to $4 million. Even finding a site for a geothermal power plant takes careful study and investigation. Often, this process also involves deep drilling to make sure there is an adequate supply of geothermal energy in the area.

Installing a geothermal heat pump is also expensive—about $7,500 for an ordinary home system. Installing a geothermal heat pump in a home that is already built requires a great deal of digging and laying of new pipes. It is a big construction project that is inconvenient to many people.

The Need for New Technology

Enhanced geothermal systems are a promising approach for geothermal energy. Using EGS, people may be able to increase the number of places where geothermal sources can be used to produce electricity. Many experts, however, say that EGS is not ready for wide use. This is in part because of the challenges

involved in drilling the deep wells needed for EGS. Most shallow geothermal wells use the same technology that is used for drilling oil and natural gas wells. The deeper wells needed for EGS present problems that old technology cannot handle.

Compared to other wells, those needed for EGS have to be drilled into harder, drier, hotter rock. One problem with drilling into very hard rock is that the drill bits (the ends of the tools) wear out quickly. Many bits used for geothermal drilling are worn out after only 50 hours of use. Some engineers are working to make new bits that use harder materials and have better designs for cutting.

There are also problems related to temperature. As wells reach deeper into Earth, temperatures increase. Standard electronic equipment cannot work in such heat. EGS drilling equipment must include special electronic monitoring devices that let operators know what is going on beneath the surface. More work needs to be done to make electronic devices that can be used on deep-drilling equipment.

In geothermal work, special geothermal drill bits are needed for drilling into very hard rock.

Possible Environmental Damage

The 2006 report on geothermal energy written by scientists from the Massachusetts Institute of Technology (MIT) was very positive. Its general view was that geothermal energy was likely to cause fewer environmental problems than many other energy sources. At the same time, the report listed some problems that could come with the use of EGS. Drilling of wells may result in the pollution of fresh water in shallow aquifers. Water that comes up through a geothermal well often contains harmful minerals. Wells need to be monitored to prevent these minerals from getting into water that people use directly.

In addition, although working geothermal power plants are not normally noisy, there is a threat of noise pollution. The sound made by the drilling and testing of wells can reach 115 **decibels** at the boundary of the site. That is about as loud as the sound of a chainsaw up close. Damage to land is another threat associated with geothermal energy. If a geothermal

Did You Know?
Geothermal Byproducts

Some geothermal power plants produce a muddy substance called sludge. Sludge from these plants contains minerals, such as zinc and sulfur, that can pollute land. If the minerals are removed from the sludge, however, they can be useful. Some geothermal plants that produce sludge treat the minerals as another product. They sell them for use in industry. This helps the plants make extra money. (The rest of the sludge must be properly disposed of.)

Sulfur is removed from sludge at a geothermal plant.

power plant brings water up to the surface faster than it injects the water back down, this can lead to a sinking of the land.

The Threat of Earthquakes

EGS requires very deep drilling into Earth. This type of drilling has the potential to disturb the balance of rock within Earth. Probably the greatest threat from this drilling is the possibility of earthquakes.

Did You Know?

Improving Drilling Technology

Engineers and scientists are experimenting with completely new drilling technologies. **Projectile** drilling uses steel balls shot with pressurized water to break up rock. A technology called spallation drilling fractures or melts rock with very hot flames. **Laser** drilling works like spallation drilling, but it uses laser pulses to heat rock. Another new technique, chemical drilling, uses strong acids to break down rock. Researchers are still working on all of these new drilling technologies. If any of these new techniques reaches the market, it might be easier to drill deep wells.

On December 8, 2006, a series of earthquakes began in Basel, Switzerland, where drilling for a new geothermal power plant was going on. First, there was a series of small **tremors**. Then, a larger quake hit. It measured 3.4 on the **Richter scale**. Earthquakes continued in Basel for about a year. Three of the later quakes also

Part of the drilling machinery in Basel, Switzerland, which was blamed for setting off earthquakes.

measured above 3 on the Richter scale. In total, more than 3,500 earthquakes were recorded in the area.

These earthquakes were very alarming because they were caused by humans. A company called Geothermal Explorers was **prospecting** for geothermal energy in Basel. The company was drilling a well that was 3 miles (5 kilometers) deep. As soon as the tremors started, company officials stopped the drilling. Fortunately, no one was hurt by the quakes. The quakes did, however, damage thousands of houses in Switzerland and nearby Germany and France. To pay for the damage, the company's insurance company paid more than $8 million. In December 2009, the Swiss government permanently shut down the project.

Did You Know?
Iceland Deep Drilling Project

The goal of the Iceland Deep Drilling Project (IDDP) is to drill a geothermal well that is 14,760 feet (4,500 meters) deep. At this depth, the inside of Earth is thought to be very hot and under very high pressure. Scientists planned to study the well during the project. They hoped to learn whether it is economical to extract energy and chemicals from such hot regions inside Earth. In June 2009, the IDDP drill hit magma at a depth of only 6,900 feet (2,100 meters) at a site in Krafla, Iceland. This was a big surprise to the researchers. According to the IDDP, hitting magma at this depth may allow for tests of EGS sooner than anticipated.

CHAPTER 5

Geothermal Tomorrow

Interest in geothermal energy is strong. In December 2008, the U.S. Bureau of Land Management opened up approximately 190 million acres (77 million hectares) of land in the western United States for geothermal exploration. U.S. President Barack Obama has spoken of the role of geothermal energy in the country's energy future. In May 2009, he announced $350 million in funding for geothermal energy projects.

Geothermal energy is also promoted by organizations such as the Geothermal Energy Association, the International Geothermal Association, and the Geo-Heat Center. These organizations hold events to help promote geothermal energy. Both governments and companies take part in these conferences. Google, the Internet search-engine company, also promotes geothermal energy. In 2008, Google invested more than $10 million in geothermal energy companies and a research lab.

100,000 Megawatts of Electricity?

The 2006 MIT report on geothermal energy said that EGS could bring huge growth in geothermal energy use in the United States. It said that in 50 years, the United States could use geothermal energy to produce 100,000 megawatts of electricity per year.

In 2008, the U.S. Department of Energy evaluated the MIT report. The Department of Energy wanted to see if pursuing geothermal energy makes economic sense. It concluded that three important things were not known for sure. First, it is not clear that big enough geothermal reservoirs can be made for commercial use. Next, hot water in EGS reservoirs does not yet flow fast or hot enough for commercial use. The Department of Energy says speeds have to be more than doubled. Finally, it is not clear that EGS can work in areas that have certain types of underground rock.

The good news, according to the Department of Energy, is that progress can be made on these issues. The limits of current

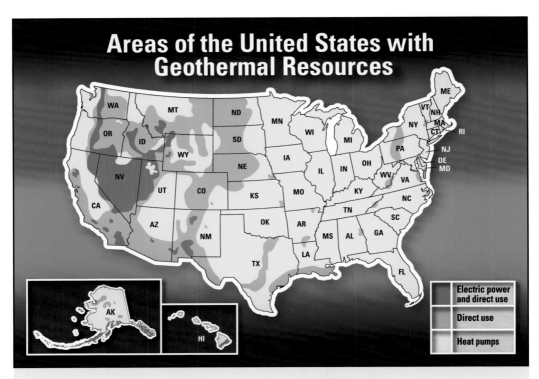

The United States has vast geothermal resources that could be used for heat pumps, direct use heating, and/or generating electricity.

A worker examines a hole drilled for geothermal exploration.

technology will not hold back research. Still, the Department of Energy stresses the need for better technology. It will likely take many improvements before EGS becomes common.

Safety Concerns

Even if these questions are answered and technology is improved, EGS may still not become widespread. In June 2009, controversy broke out over EGS drilling in California. A company called AltaRock Energy was about to begin drilling for geothermal energy. AltaRock was planning to use the same drilling techniques that had caused earthquakes in Basel, Switzerland. The site at which AltaRock planned to drill was close to the Geysers. The region is known to produce

At a fish farm in Israel, ponds are filled with geothermal water from under the Negev Desert.

a great deal of geothermal energy, but it is also known for earthquakes. Many people worried that drilling deep into the ground there and fracturing the rock below was too dangerous.

In July, the Department of Energy and the Bureau of Land Management told AltaRock that it could not proceed with fracturing rock until they reviewed its plans. AltaRock was allowed to proceed with drilling. In August, however, the drilling project began having problems. At one point, a drill bit snapped off. The project also fell far behind schedule. In early September 2009, AltaRock stopped the project. Three months later, the company removed its drill rig from the area and told the government that it would not be continuing work there.

Here To Stay

Whatever happens with EGS, geothermal energy is in the United States to stay. The Geothermal Energy Association reports that between 50,000 and 60,000 geothermal heat pumps are installed each year in the United States. If people can afford the cost of installation, they stand to save a lot of money in the long run.

Many states are working to develop geothermal power plants to produce electricity. As of

AltaRock Energy's drilling project in California, called off in late 2009.

PEOPLE TO KNOW

SUSAN PETTY

Susan Petty is the president and one of the founders of AltaRock, a company that is working to develop resources for geothermal energy in the United States. "Our goal is to get to where we can develop geothermal anywhere," she says. Petty graduated from Princeton University in 1973. She received a master's degree in **hydrology** from the University of Hawaii in 1980. She worked as a geologist and scientist on many projects around the world. Before she founded AltaRock, Petty was a member of a company that gives advice about geothermal energy. She was also a member of the group of experts who wrote MIT's 2006 report on geothermal energy. AltaRock, her current company, specializes in EGS and works on developing new technologies that will help make EGS less expensive.

August 2008, 13 states—Alaska, Arizona, California, Colorado, Florida, Hawaii, Idaho, Nevada, New Mexico, Oregon, Utah, Washington, and Wyoming—had new geothermal energy projects in the works. These projects have the potential to generate 4,000 megawatts of electricity.

The use of geothermal energy will also likely continue to grow around the world. The International Geothermal Association estimates that world geothermal capacity could rise to 11,000 megawatts by 2010, from 9,065 megawatts in 2005. More countries in North

In this Colorado greenhouse, tomatoes are grown with water from geothermal wells.

Did You Know?
Careers in Geothermal Energy

The U.S. Department of Energy says that the geothermal energy industry requires workers with many different skills. Geologists, geochemists, geophysicists, **hydrologists**, reservoir engineers, **hydraulic** engineers, and mud loggers work on developing geothermal reservoirs. (Mud loggers are people who analyze the drilling fluids, which are called "mud," that come from a well.) Finding sites for geothermal development requires environmental scientists to study the impact of development. When a site is found, specialists work to secure the rights to use the land. Power plants need electrical and mechanical engineers. Building the plants requires many construction workers, electricians, welders, and mechanics.

Even smaller scale use of geothermal energy requires many types of workers. Heating engineers design geothermal systems for buildings and the agricultural industry. Making and installing geothermal heat pumps requires engineers, geologists, drilling crews, and contractors. Engineers, geologists, chemists, and materials scientists are needed to develop new technology.

America, South America, Europe, Asia, and Africa may begin to produce electricity with geothermal energy. It may take a long time until the heat inside Earth is a major source of power for people living on the planet, but people will likely make greater use of this clean, renewable resource.

GLOSSARY

acid rain: Rain, snow, fog, or mist that contains acid substances and damages the environment.

antifreeze: A chemical that is added to liquid that raises the liquid's freezing point.

aquifer: A layer of rock, sand, or gravel beneath Earth's surface that contains water.

atmosphere: The envelope of air that surrounds the planet.

biofuels: Renewable fuels that come from living things.

carbon dioxide: A gas formed when fossil fuels are burned; also written as CO_2.

catastrophe: A tragic event or disaster.

climate: The weather and overall conditions in a place as measured over a long period of time.

controversial: Causing many arguments or open to debate.

core: The very hot center of Earth.

decibel: A unit used to measure the volume of sounds.

developing country: A relatively poor, unindustrialized country.

device: Something that does some action.

district: An area or region of a city.

emission: A substance that is released into the air.

fossil fuels: Fuels, such as coal, natural gas, or oil, that were formed underground over millions of years from the remains of prehistoric plants and animals. Such fuels are not renewable.

generator: A machine that is used to convert energy, such as that provided by burning fuel or by wind or water, into electricity.

geyser: A spring that naturally shoots hot water and steam into the air.

hot spring: A spring of water that is heated by Earth's interior.

hydraulic: Related to devices that work when liquid is forced under pressure through pipes.

hydrologist: Someone involved with hydrology.

hydrology: The study of the properties and use of the water on Earth and in the atmosphere.

laser: A device that produces a focused beam of radiation.

magma: Molten rock beneath Earth's surface.

mantle: The part of Earth that lies beneath the crust and above the core.

megawatt: A million watts. A watt is a common unit of measurement for the rate at which electric energy is used.

nuclear: Having to do with nuclear energy, created by splitting atoms.

plate: A section of Earth's crust and upper mantle that is constantly moving very slowly.

power plant: A place for the production of electric power, also sometimes called a "power station."

projectile: An object that is moved forward by an external force.

prospecting: Exploring an area in search of a substance, such as underground water or mineral deposits.

radioactive waste: Materials that give off harmful radiation, or radioactivity, and are left over from the production of nuclear power.

renewable: A resource that never gets used up. Energy sources such as sunlight and wind are renewable; sources such as coal, natural gas, and oil are nonrenewable.

reservoir: A naturally occurring underground body of water.

Richter scale: A scale for measuring the severity of earthquakes.

rotor: A part of a machine that turns.

sustainable: Able to last and not be used up. The word is often used with regard to ways of living and working that leave plenty of natural resources for the future.

tremor: A shaking movement.

turbine: A machine that produces a turning action, which can be used to make electricity. The turning action may be caused by steam, wind, or some other energy source.

vapor: Particles of moisture in the air in the form of steam, clouds, fumes, or smoke.

TO LEARN MORE

Read these books:

Fridell, Ron. *Earth-Friendly Energy*. Minneapolis: Lerner Publications, 2009.

Gleason, Carrie. *Geothermal Energy: Using Earth's Furnace*. New York: Crabtree Publishing Company, 2008.

Morgan, Sally. *Alternative Energy Sources*. Chicago: Heinemann Library, 2009.

Savage, Lorraine. *Geothermal Power*. Farmington Hills, Michigan: Greenhaven Press, 2006.

Look up these Web sites:

EIA Energy Kids—Geothermal Energy
http://tonto.eia.doe.gov/kids/energy.cfm?page = geothermal_home

Energy Story: Geothermal Energy
http://www.energyquest.ca.gov/story/chapter11.html

Geothermal Energy Association
http://www.geo-energy.org

Geothermal Energy 101
http://www.digtheheat.com/geothermal/geothermalbasics.html

Geothermal Technologies Program
http://www1.eere.energy.gov/geothermal/index.html

How Geothermal Energy Works
http://www.howstuffworks.com/geothermal-energy.htm

Key Internet search terms:

EGS, geothermal, geyser, hot spring, renewable energy

INDEX

The abbreviation *ill.* stands for illustration, and *ills.* stands for illustrations. Page references to illustrations and maps are in *italic* type.

Acid rain 29
Advantages of geothermal energy 24–31
Alaska 8, 24
AltaRock Energy 40, 41, 42; *ill. 41*
Animals and plants 8, 9; *ill. 40*
Aquifers 23, 34
Arizona 42; *ill. 33*
Atmosphere 10, 31

Basel (Switzerland) 36–37, 40; *ill. 36*
Binary-cycle plants 20, 21–22, 31; *ill. 19*
Biofuels 6; *ill. 11*
Businesses 13; *ill. 42*

Carbon dioxide 10, 29, 31
Climate change 10
Coal 8, 9; *ills. 10, 11*
Colorado 23; *ills. 22, 42*
Colter, John 12, 16
Conti, Prince Piero Ginori 17
Cooling *see* Heating and cooling
Core (geology) 4; *ill. 5*
Costs 27, 29, 32

Demand for energy 5, 7, 8, 11, 30
Department of Energy, U.S. 39, 40, 41, 43

Direct use 5–6, 14, 15, 16, 23, 25
District heating 13, 23
Drawbacks of geothermal energy 32–37
Drilling and installation 22, 29, 32; *ills. 36, 40, 41*
environmental problems 34–35, 36–37
safety concerns 40, 41
technology for 33, 36
Dry-steam plants 18, 20; *ill. 19*

Earth (planet) 4, 10, 15, 24, 26; *ill. 5*
Earthquakes 26, 35–37, 41
Economic benefits 27, 29
Electricity 5, 6, 8, 14, 15, 17, 20, 38
production methods 18–22; *ill. 19*
Enhanced geothermal systems (EGS) 21, 22, 25, 32–34, 38
earthquakes, threat of 35, 36

improvements, need for 39, 40
Environmental issues 29, 31, 34–35
Flash-steam plants 20, 21, 31; *ill. 19*
Fossil fuels 8–11, 29, 31
Future developments 11, 38–42

Geysers 4, 9; *ill. 6*
Geysers (California) 12, 13, 14, 15, 27, 31, 40; *ill. 27*
Global warming 10, 29

Hawaii 24, 42
Heat exchanger 14, 16, 21
Heat-pump systems 14, 15, 18, 25, 27, 29, 32, 41
Heating and cooling 5, 6, 12, 13, 14, 18, 22–23, 25
costs of 27, 29
Historic development 12–14, 17
Homes and buildings 5, 6, 13, 16, 17; *ills. 25, 28*
costs of heating 27, 29
heat pumps, use of 18, 23

Hot springs 4, 12, 13, 16, 31; *ill. 13*
Hot Springs National Park (Arkansas) 12; *ill. 13*

Iceland 6, 20, 37; *ill. 7*
Iceland Deep Drilling Project 37
Italy 6, 12, 14, 17; *ill. 17*

Jobs and careers 29, 43

Klamath Falls (Oregon) 23; *ill. 23*

Land Management, Bureau of, U.S. 38, 41
Larderello (Italy) 14, 17, 27; *ill. 17*
Lieb, Charlie 14

Magma 4, 24, 26, 37; *ills. 5, 7*
Mantle (geology) 4, 24; *ill. 5*
Massachusetts Institute of Technology (MIT) 11, 34, 38, 39, 42
Minerals 34, 35

Need for alternative energy 7–11
New York 23, 24, 28

New Zealand 6, 20; *ill. 6*
Nielsen, Carl 14
Nuclear power 9, 11; *ill. 11*

Obama, Barack 38
Oil and natural gas 8, 9, 30, 31; *ill. 11*
Old Faithful (geyser) 9
OPEC (Organization of Petroleum Exporting Countries) 30
Ouray Hot Springs Pool (Colorado) 23; *ill. 22*

Papua New Guinea 20
Petty, Susan 42
Philippines, the 6, 20, 24
Pollution 9, 29, 31, 34, 35; *ill. 10*
Power plants 9, 13, 14, 15, 17, 25, 27; *ills. 17, 27, 31*
environmental issues 31, 34, 35
types of 18–22; *ill. 19*

Research and experimentation 8, 21, 22, 36, 37

trends in 41, 42
Reservoirs 16, 21, 39
Resorts and spas 8, 12–13
Resources, availability of 24; *map 39*
Ring of Fire 26; *map 26*

Sludge 35
Sources of energy 8; *ill. 11*

Tectonic plates 24, 26
Temperature 4, 9, 10, 16, 18, 20, 21, 24, 25, 38
Turbines 18, 20, 21; *ill. 19*

United States 6, 8, 9, 24, 30, 38; *ill. 11, map 39*
economic benefits to 29
oil import 30
Use of energy 5–7, 11, 12–14, 22–23

Volcanoes 4, 17, 24, 26; *ill. 6*

Yellowstone National Park (Wyoming-Montana-Idaho) 9, 12, 16

About the Author

Alan Wachtel is a New York–based writer and editor. He has worked on nonfiction educational books for children and young adults since 2001. Topics he has written on include science, history, and current affairs.